This Journal Belongs to:
_____

ISBN 978-0-9912323-6-9
Around the World in Style: The Travel Journal
2015 © Ariana Pierce

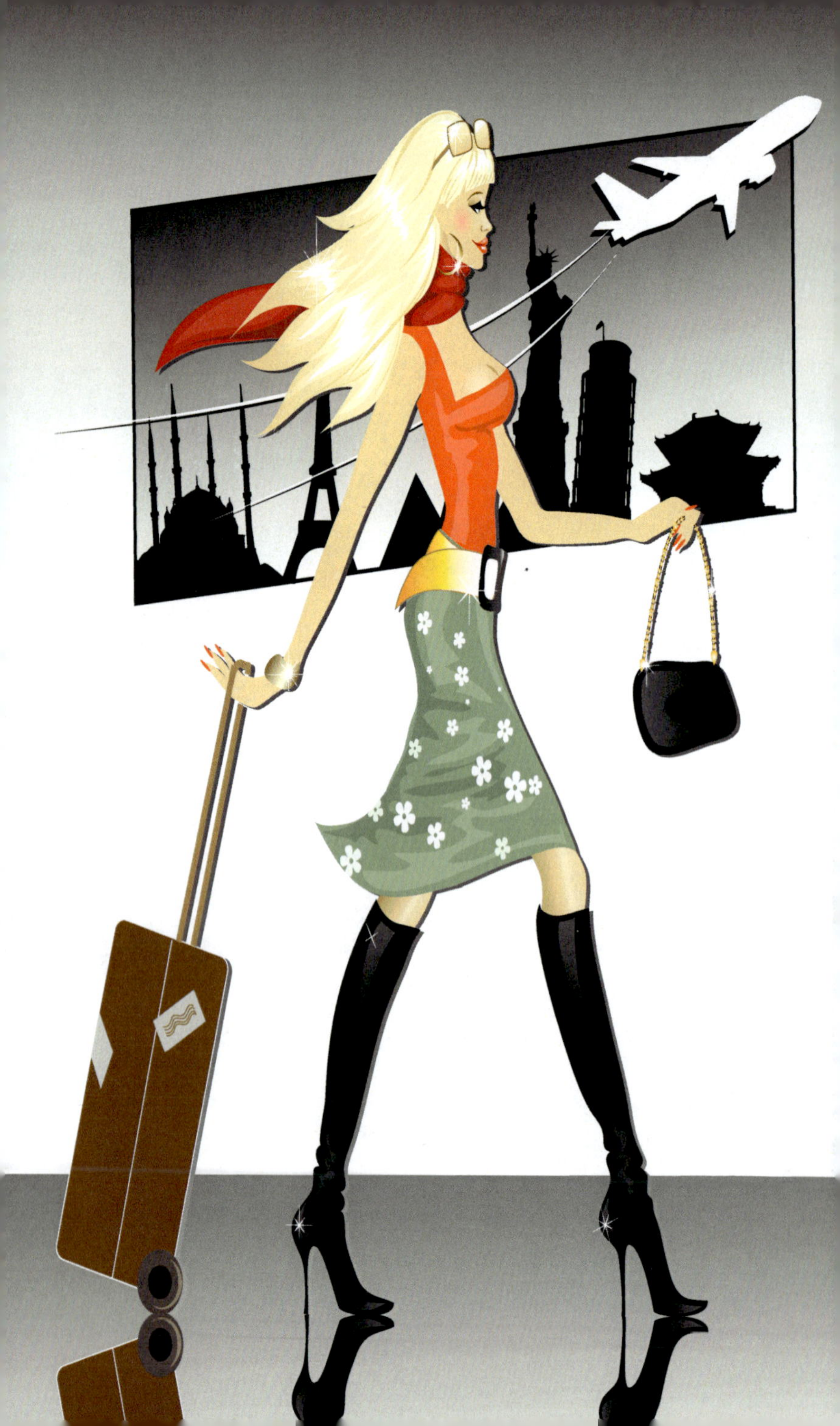

Around the World in Style ©Ariana Pierce

"To travel is to take a journey into yourself." – Danny Kaye

Show me the right path, O Lord, point out the road for me to follow.
Psalm 25:4

Around the World in Style ©Ariana Pierce

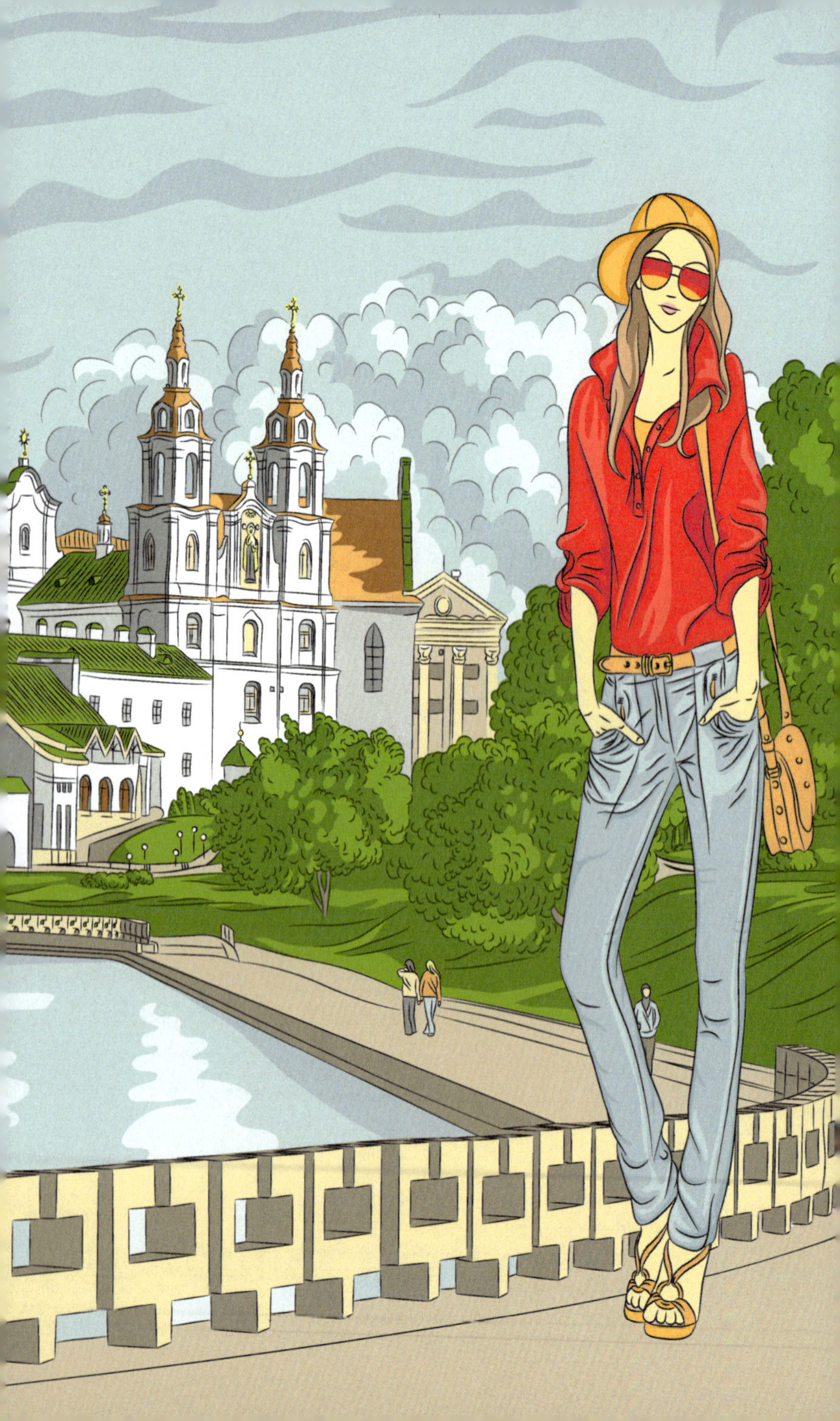

Around the World in Style ©Ariana Pierce

My Trip Details

Use the space below to write the details about a trip you've enjoyed.

Destination: _____ **Travel Date:** _____

Itinerary

Airline Used

Hotel

Restaurants

Notes

Sites I Saw

Places I Went

Memorable
Moments

My Awesome
Adventures

Around the World in Style ©Ariana Pierce

My Dream Trip Vision Page

Use the space provided to paste pictures of your dream travel destination. Include places you'd like to visit, things you'd like to see and enjoy.

Destination: _____

Around the World in Style ©Ariana Pierce

Packing List

Destination: _____ **Date:** _____

Clothing

Accessories
- ☐ Belts
- ☐ Glasses & case
- ☐ Jewelry
- ☐ Sunglasses
- ☐ Ties
- ☐ Wristwatches

Basics
- ☐ Bras
- ☐ Pantyhose
- ☐ Robe
- ☐ Sleepwear
- ☐ Socks
- ☐ Tanks
- ☐ Undershirts
- ☐ Underwear

Casual
- ☐ Exercise wear
- ☐ Jeans
- ☐ Pants
- ☐ Shirts
- ☐ Shorts
- ☐ Swimsuits
- ☐ Tshirts

Dressy
- ☐ Dresses
- ☐ Dress shirts
- ☐ Skirts
- ☐ Suits
- ☐ Sweaters
- ☐ Tuxedo

Footwear
- ☐ Athletic
- ☐ Leisure
- ☐ Dress
- ☐ Sandals/Flip flops
- ☐ Slippers

Outerwear
- ☐ Coats
- ☐ Jackets
- ☐ Gloves
- ☐ Hats
- ☐ Raincoat
- ☐ Scarves

Hygiene

Toiletries
- ☐ Bath gel
- ☐ Birth control
- ☐ Brush
- ☐ Comb
- ☐ Conditioner
- ☐ Contact Lenses & case
- ☐ Cotton balls
- ☐ Cotton swabs
- ☐ Curling Iron/Flat Iron
- ☐ Dental floss
- ☐ Deodorant
- ☐ Feminine Hygiene
- ☐ Hair dryer
- ☐ Insect repellent
- ☐ Lint roller
- ☐ Lip balm
- ☐ Medications
- ☐ Mirror
- ☐ Moisturizer
- ☐ Mouthwash
- ☐ Pain reliever
- ☐ Perfume
- ☐ Razor
- ☐ Saline solution
- ☐ Shampoo
- ☐ Sunscreen/block
- ☐ Tissue
- ☐ Toothbrush
- ☐ Toothpaste
- ☐ Tweezers
- ☐ Vitamins

Makeup
- ☐ Face cleanser
- ☐ Hand wipes
- ☐ Lip stick
- ☐ Makeup
- ☐ Nail clippers
- ☐ Nail file
- ☐ Nail polish
- ☐ Nail polish remover

Basic

Travel Aids
- ☐ Anxiety medication
- ☐ Bottled water
- ☐ Chewing gum
- ☐ Motion-sickness remedy
- ☐ Pleasure reading
- ☐ Sleeping mask
- ☐ Travel pillow
- ☐ Snacks

Other
- ☐ Directions
- ☐ First Aid Kit
- ☐ Journal
- ☐ Luggage tags
- ☐ Reservation info.
- ☐ Tickets
- ☐ Travel guides
- ☐ Travel locks
- Umbrella

Funds
- ☐ ATM card
- ☐ Cash
- ☐ Credit cards
- ☐ Money belt
- ☐ Plastic bags
- ☐ Travelers Checks
- ☐ Wallet

Around the World in Style ©Ariana Pierce

Packing List Continued

Tech Tools
- ☐ Batteries
- ☐ Battery/Juice Pack
- ☐ Car Charger
- ☐ Camera
- ☐ Camera Charger
- ☐ Cell phone
- ☐ Cell phone Charger
- ☐ Extension Cord
- ☐ Headphones
- ☐ Laptop
- ☐ Laptop Cord
- ☐ Nightlight
- ☐ Powerstrip
- ☐ Printer
- ☐ Tablet
- ☐ Tablet Cord
- ☐ Wall Jacks
- ☐ Voltage Adapters
- ☐ _____
- ☐ _____
- ☐ _____
- ☐ _____
- ☐ _____

Survival Kit
- ☐ Bobby Pins
- ☐ Business Cards
- ☐ Deoderant
- ☐ Eyelash Glue
- ☐ Flat shoes
- ☐ Magazine
- ☐ Note pad
- ☐ Pens
- ☐ Safety Pins
- ☐ Sewing Kit (small)
- ☐ Silk Hair Bonnet
- ☐ Silk Pillow Case (hair)
- ☐ Sticky Notes

Keep this kit packed and ready for travel at a moments notice.

Misc

Documents
- ☐ Copies of travel docs
- ☐ Copies of credit cards
- ☐ Copies of passport
- ☐ Drivers License
- ☐ Emergency contacts
- ☐ Medical cards
- ☐ Medical history
- ☐ List of Medications
- ☐ Passport & visas

Contacts
- ☐ Address book
- ☐ Business cards
- ☐ Calling cards
- ☐ Datebook

Laundry
- ☐ Laundry bag
- ☐ Laundry kit
- ☐ Sewing kit
- ☐ Stain remover
- ☐ Travel iron

Work
- ☐ Office Supplies
- ☐ Printer
- ☐ Work documents
- ☐ Work reading

Travel To-Do List

1.
2.
3.
4.
5.
6.
7.
8.
9.
10.
11.
12.
13.
14.
15.
16.

Notes & Ideas

Around the World in Style ©Ariana Pierce

Put your hope in the Lord. Travel steadily along His path.
Psalm 37:34 NLT

Around the World in Style ©Ariana Pierce

Milan
Milan
Milan
Milan
Milan
Milan
Milan
Milan
Milan
Milan

Around the World in Style ©Ariana Pierce

"Do not follow where the path may lead. Go instead where there is no path and leave a trail." - Ralph Waldo Emerson

Around the World in Style ©Ariana Pierce

5 days
25 km
5×25=125 km

Around the World in Style ©Ariana Pierce

5 days
25 km
5×25=125 km

"If you don't know where you're going, any road will get you there."
- Lewis Carroll

Around the World in Style ©Ariana Pierce

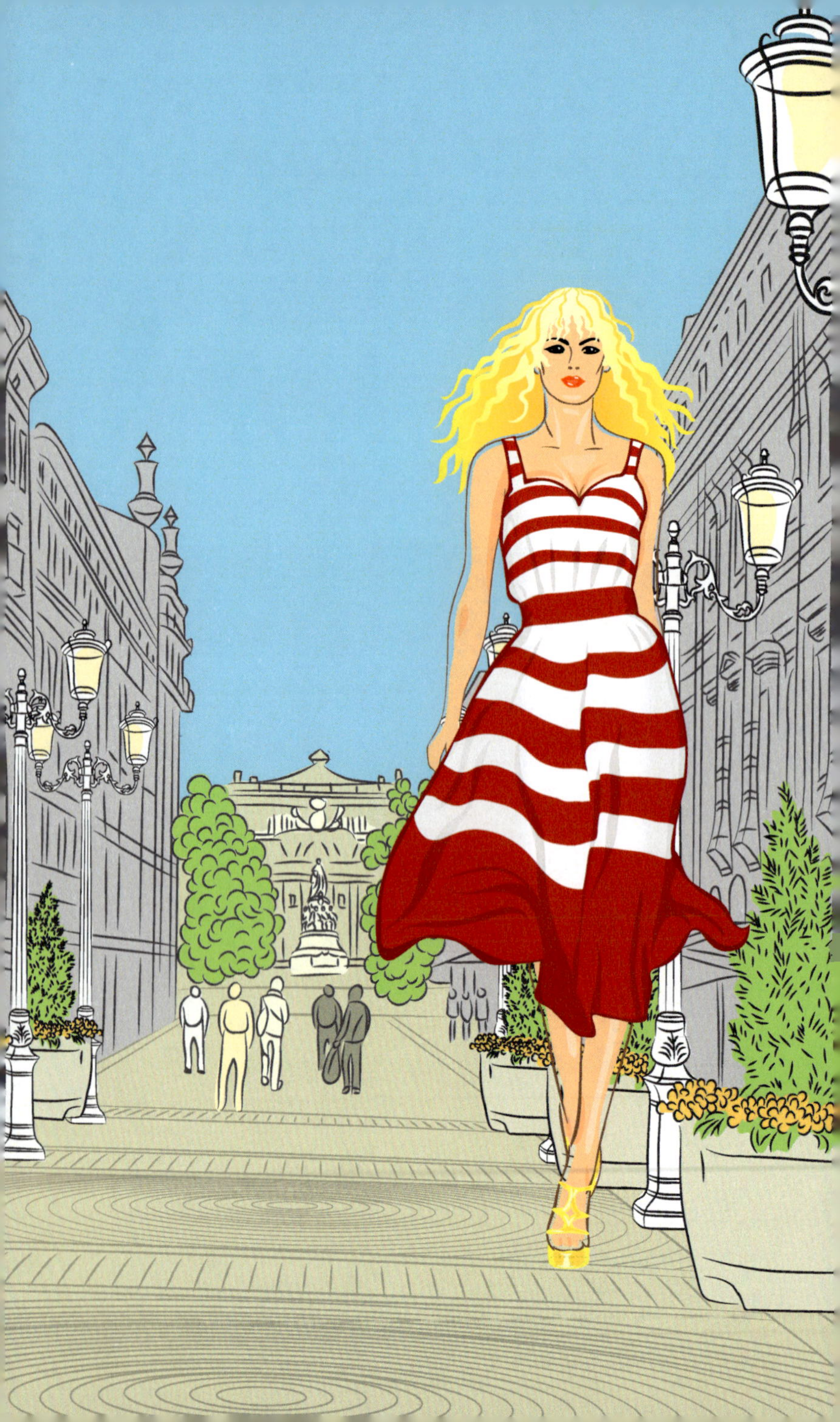

Around the World in Style ©Ariana Pierce

The Lord keeps watch over you as you come and go, both now and forever. Psalm 121:8 NLT

Around the World in Style ©Ariana Pierce

My Trip Details

Use the space below to write the details about a trip you've enjoyed.

Destination: _____ **Travel Date:** _____

Itinerary

Airline Used

Hotel

Restaurants

Notes

Sites I Saw

Places I Went

Memorable Moments

My Awesome Adventures

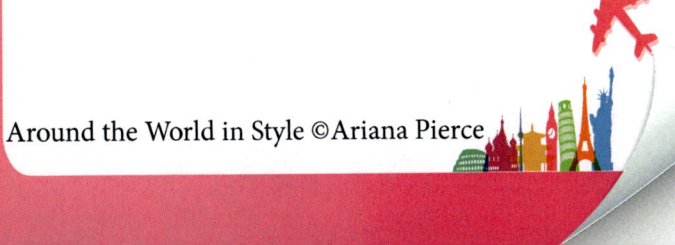

Around the World in Style ©Ariana Pierce

My Trip Scrapbook Page

Use the space provided to paste pictures and memorabilia of a travel destination you've visited.

Destination:_____

Around the World in Style ©Ariana Pierce

Packing List

Destination:_____ Date: _____

Clothing

Accessories
- ☐ Belts
- ☐ Glasses & case
- ☐ Jewelry
- ☐ Sunglasses
- ☐ Ties
- ☐ Wristwatches

Basics
- ☐ Bras
- ☐ Pantyhose
- ☐ Robe

- ☐ Sleepwear
- ☐ Socks
- ☐ Tanks
- ☐ Undershirts
- ☐ Underwear

Casual
- ☐ Exercise wear
- ☐ Jeans
- ☐ Pants
- ☐ Shirts
- ☐ Shorts
- ☐ Swimsuits

- ☐ Tshirts

Dressy
- ☐ Dresses
- ☐ Dress shirts
- ☐ Skirts
- ☐ Suits
- ☐ Sweaters
- ☐ Tuxedo

Footwear
- ☐ Athletic
- ☐ Leisure

- ☐ Dress
- ☐ Sandals/Flip flops
- ☐ Slippers

Outerwear
- ☐ Coats
- ☐ Jackets
- ☐ Gloves
- ☐ Hats
- ☐ Raincoat
- ☐ Scarves

Hygiene

Toiletries
- ☐ Bath gel
- ☐ Birth control
- ☐ Brush
- ☐ Comb
- ☐ Conditioner
- ☐ Contact Lenses & case
- ☐ Cotton balls
- ☐ Cotton swabs
- ☐ Curling Iron/Flat Iron

- ☐ Dental floss
- ☐ Deodorant
- ☐ Feminine Hygiene
- ☐ Hair dryer
- ☐ Insect repellent
- ☐ Lint roller
- ☐ Lip balm
- ☐ Medications
- ☐ Mirror
- ☐ Moisturizer
- ☐ Mouthwash

- ☐ Pain reliever
- ☐ Perfume
- ☐ Razor
- ☐ Saline solution
- ☐ Shampoo
- ☐ Sunscreen/block
- ☐ Tissue
- ☐ Toothbrush
- ☐ Toothpaste
- ☐ Tweezers
- ☐ Vitamins

Makeup
- ☐ Face cleanser
- ☐ Hand wipes
- ☐ Lip stick
- ☐ Makeup
- ☐ Nail clippers
- ☐ Nail file
- ☐ Nail polish
- ☐ Nail polish remover

Basic

Travel Aids
- ☐ Anxiety medication
- ☐ Bottled water
- ☐ Chewing gum
- ☐ Motion-sickness remedy
- ☐ Pleasure reading
- ☐ Sleeping mask
- ☐ Travel pillow
- ☐ Snacks

Other
- ☐ Directions
- ☐ First Aid Kit
- ☐ Journal
- ☐ Luggage tags
- ☐ Reservation info.
- ☐ Tickets
- ☐ Travel guides
- ☐ Travel locks
- Umbrella

Funds
- ☐ ATM card
- ☐ Cash
- ☐ Credit cards
- ☐ Money belt
- ☐ Plastic bags
- ☐ Travelers Checks
- ☐ Wallet

Around the World in Style ©Ariana Pierce

Packing List Continued

Tech Tools
- ☐ Batteries
- ☐ Battery/Juice Pack
- ☐ Car Charger
- ☐ Camera
- ☐ Camera Charger
- ☐ Cell phone
- ☐ Cell phone Charger
- ☐ Extension Cord
- ☐ Headphones
- ☐ Laptop
- ☐ Laptop Cord
- ☐ Nightlight
- ☐ Powerstrip
- ☐ Printer
- ☐ Tablet
- ☐ Tablet Cord
- ☐ Wall Jacks
- ☐ Voltage Adapters
- ☐ _____
- ☐ _____
- ☐ _____
- ☐ _____
- ☐ _____

Survival Kit
- ☐ Bobby Pins
- ☐ Business Cards
- ☐ Deoderant
- ☐ Eyelash Glue
- ☐ Flat shoes
- ☐ Magazine
- ☐ Note pad
- ☐ Pens
- ☐ Safety Pins
- ☐ Sewing Kit (small)
- ☐ Silk Hair Bonnet
- ☐ Silk Pillow Case (hair)
- ☐ Sticky Notes

Keep this kit packed and ready for travel at a moments notice.

Misc

Documents
- ☐ Copies of travel docs
- ☐ Copies of credit cards
- ☐ Copies of passport
- ☐ Drivers License
- ☐ Emergency contacts
- ☐ Medical cards
- ☐ Medical history
- ☐ List of Medications
- ☐ Passport & visas

Contacts
- ☐ Address book
- ☐ Business cards
- ☐ Calling cards
- ☐ Datebook

Laundry
- ☐ Laundry bag
- ☐ Laundry kit
- ☐ Sewing kit
- ☐ Stain remover
- ☐ Travel iron

Work
- ☐ Office Supplies
- ☐ Printer
- ☐ Work documents
- ☐ Work reading

Travel To-Do List

1.
2.
3.
4.
5.
6.
7.
8.
9.
10.
11.
12.
13.
14.
15.
16.

Notes & Ideas

Around the World in Style ©Ariana Pierce

"The journey of a thousand miles begins with a single step."
-Lao Tzu

Around the World in Style ©Ariana Pierce

5 days
25 km
5×25=125km

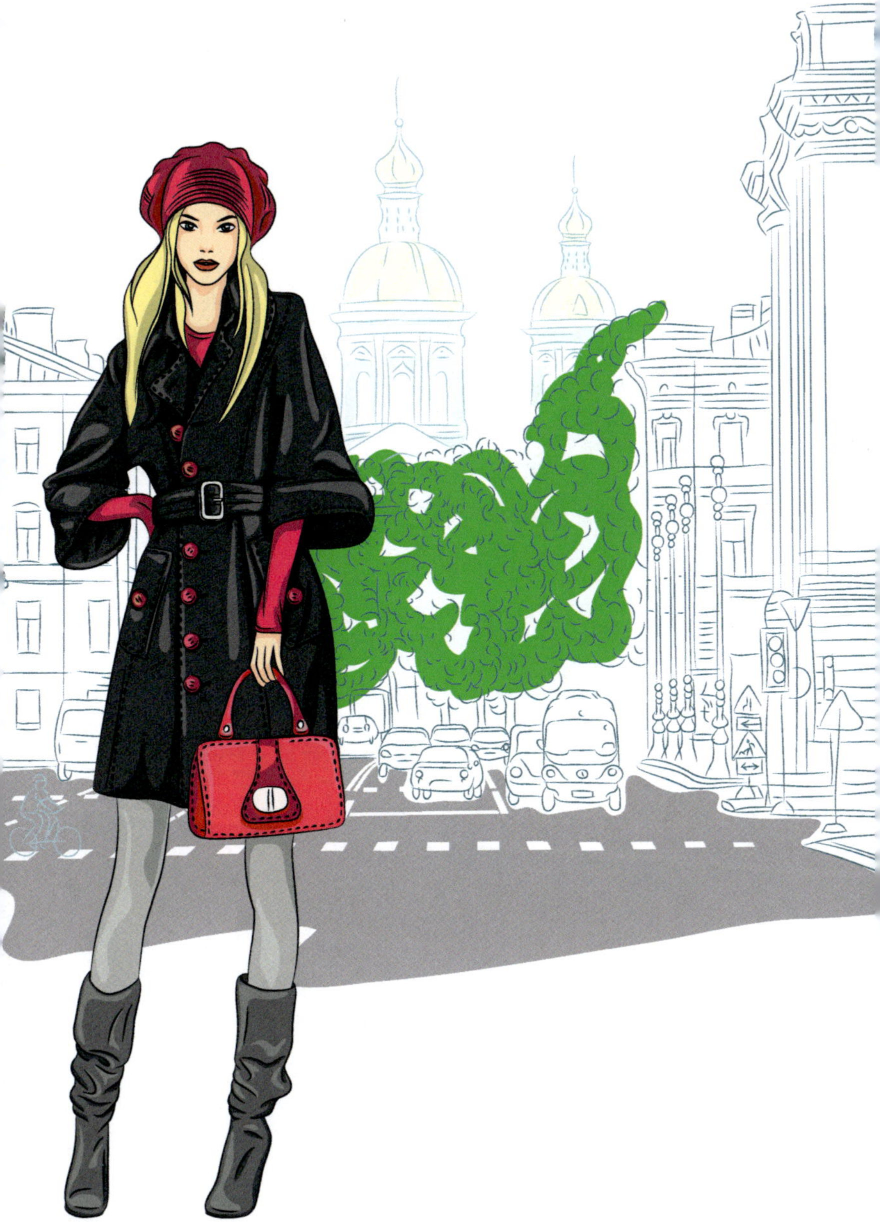

"The World is a book, and those who do not travel read only a page."
– Saint Augustine

Around the World in Style ©Ariana Pierce

My Dream Trip Details

Use the space below to write the details about a trip you would like to take.

Destination: _____   **Travel Date:** _____

Itinerary

Airline Used

Hotel

Restaurants

Notes

Sites to See

Places to Go

Memorable Moments

My Awesome Adventures

Around the World in Style ©Ariana Pierce

My Dream Trip Vision Page

Use the space provided to paste pictures of your dream travel destination. Include places you'd like to visit, things you'd like to see and enjoy.

Destination:_____

Around the World in Style ©Ariana Pierce

Packing List

Destination: _____ Date: _____

Clothing

Accessories
- ☐ Belts
- ☐ Glasses & case
- ☐ Jewelry
- ☐ Sunglasses
- ☐ Ties
- ☐ Wristwatches

Basics
- ☐ Bras
- ☐ Pantyhose
- ☐ Robe
- ☐ Sleepwear
- ☐ Socks
- ☐ Tanks
- ☐ Undershirts
- ☐ Underwear

Casual
- ☐ Exercise wear
- ☐ Jeans
- ☐ Pants
- ☐ Shirts
- ☐ Shorts
- ☐ Swimsuits
- ☐ Tshirts

Dressy
- ☐ Dresses
- ☐ Dress shirts
- ☐ Skirts
- ☐ Suits
- ☐ Sweaters
- ☐ Tuxedo

Footwear
- ☐ Athletic
- ☐ Leisure
- ☐ Dress
- ☐ Sandals/Flip flops
- ☐ Slippers

Outerwear
- ☐ Coats
- ☐ Jackets
- ☐ Gloves
- ☐ Hats
- ☐ Raincoat
- ☐ Scarves

Hygiene

Toiletries
- ☐ Bath gel
- ☐ Birth control
- ☐ Brush
- ☐ Comb
- ☐ Conditioner
- ☐ Contact Lenses & case
- ☐ Cotton balls
- ☐ Cotton swabs
- ☐ Curling Iron/Flat Iron
- ☐ Dental floss
- ☐ Deodorant
- ☐ Feminine Hygiene
- ☐ Hair dryer
- ☐ Insect repellent
- ☐ Lint roller
- ☐ Lip balm
- ☐ Medications
- ☐ Mirror
- ☐ Moisturizer
- ☐ Mouthwash
- ☐ Pain reliever
- ☐ Perfume
- ☐ Razor
- ☐ Saline solution
- ☐ Shampoo
- ☐ Sunscreen/block
- ☐ Tissue
- ☐ Toothbrush
- ☐ Toothpaste
- ☐ Tweezers
- ☐ Vitamins

Makeup
- ☐ Face cleanser
- ☐ Hand wipes
- ☐ Lip stick
- ☐ Makeup
- ☐ Nail clippers
- ☐ Nail file
- ☐ Nail polish
- ☐ Nail polish remover

Basic

Travel Aids
- ☐ Anxiety medication
- ☐ Bottled water
- ☐ Chewing gum
- ☐ Motion-sickness remedy
- ☐ Pleasure reading
- ☐ Sleeping mask
- ☐ Travel pillow
- ☐ Snacks

Other
- ☐ Directions
- ☐ First Aid Kit
- ☐ Journal
- ☐ Luggage tags
- ☐ Reservation info.
- ☐ Tickets
- ☐ Travel guides
- ☐ Travel locks
- ☐ Umbrella

Funds
- ☐ ATM card
- ☐ Cash
- ☐ Credit cards
- ☐ Money belt
- ☐ Plastic bags
- ☐ Travelers Checks
- ☐ Wallet

Around the World in Style ©Ariana Pierce

Packing List Continued

Tech Tools
- ☐ Batteries
- ☐ Battery/Juice Pack
- ☐ Car Charger
- ☐ Camera
- ☐ Camera Charger
- ☐ Cell phone
- ☐ Cell phone Charger
- ☐ Extension Cord
- ☐ Headphones
- ☐ Laptop
- ☐ Laptop Cord
- ☐ Nightlight
- ☐ Powerstrip
- ☐ Printer
- ☐ Tablet
- ☐ Tablet Cord
- ☐ Wall Jacks
- ☐ Voltage Adapters
- ☐ _____
- ☐ _____
- ☐ _____
- ☐ _____
- ☐ _____

Survival Kit
- ☐ Bobby Pins
- ☐ Business Cards
- ☐ Deodorant
- ☐ Eyelash Glue
- ☐ Flat shoes
- ☐ Magazine
- ☐ Note pad
- ☐ Pens
- ☐ Safety Pins
- ☐ Sewing Kit (small)
- ☐ Silk Hair Bonnet
- ☐ Silk Pillow Case (hair)
- ☐ Sticky Notes

Keep this kit packed and ready for travel at a moments notice.

Misc

Documents
- ☐ Copies of travel docs
- ☐ Copies of credit cards
- ☐ Copies of passport
- ☐ Drivers License
- ☐ Emergency contacts
- ☐ Medical cards
- ☐ Medical history
- ☐ List of Medications
- ☐ Passport & visas

Contacts
- ☐ Address book
- ☐ Business cards
- ☐ Calling cards
- ☐ Datebook

Laundry
- ☐ Laundry bag
- ☐ Laundry kit
- ☐ Sewing kit
- ☐ Stain remover
- ☐ Travel iron

Work
- ☐ Office Supplies
- ☐ Printer
- ☐ Work documents
- ☐ Work reading

Travel To-Do List

1.
2.
3.
4.
5.
6.
7.
8.
9.
10.
11.
12.
13.
14.
15.
16.

Notes & Ideas

Around the World in Style ©Ariana Pierce

I want you to get out there and walk, better yet run, on the road God called you to travel. Eph 4:1 MSG

Around the World in Style ©Ariana Pierce

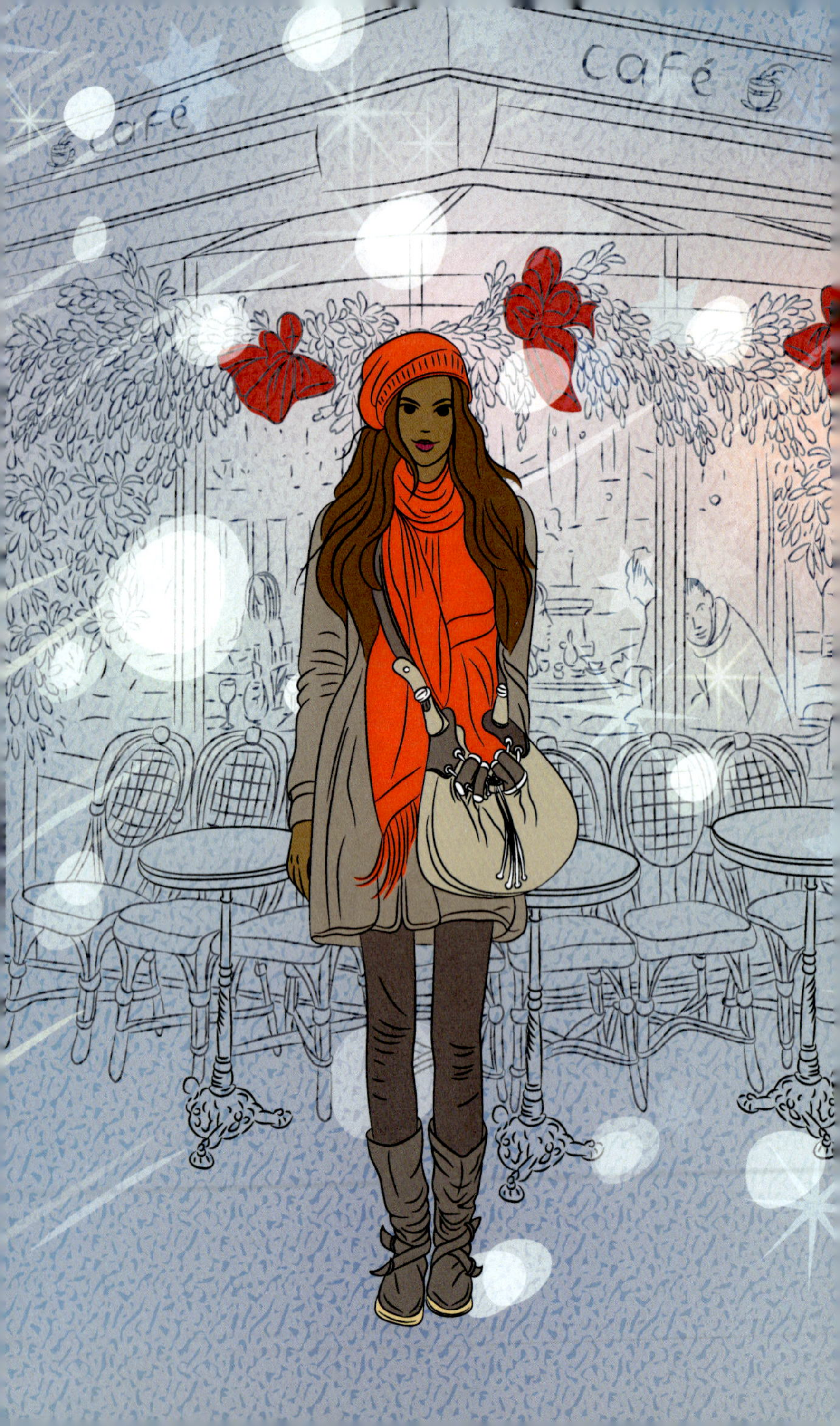
Café
Café

Around the World in Style ©Ariana Pierce

Around the World in Style ©Ariana Pierce

My Trip Details

Use the space below to write the details about a trip you've enjoyed.

Destination: _____ **Travel Date:** _____

Itinerary

Airline Used

Hotel

Restaurants

Notes

Sites I Saw

Places I Went

Memorable Moments

My Awesome Adventures

Around the World in Style ©Ariana Pierce

My Trip Scrapbook Page

Use the space provided to paste pictures and memorabilia of a travel destination you've visited.

Destination:

Around the World in Style ©Ariana Pierce

Packing List

Destination: _____ **Date:** _____

Clothing

Accessories
- ☐ Belts
- ☐ Glasses & case
- ☐ Jewelry
- ☐ Sunglasses
- ☐ Ties
- ☐ Wristwatches

Basics
- ☐ Bras
- ☐ Pantyhose
- ☐ Robe

- ☐ Sleepwear
- ☐ Socks
- ☐ Tanks
- ☐ Undershirts
- ☐ Underwear

Casual
- ☐ Exercise wear
- ☐ Jeans
- ☐ Pants
- ☐ Shirts
- ☐ Shorts
- ☐ Swimsuits

- ☐ Tshirts

Dressy
- ☐ Dresses
- ☐ Dress shirts
- ☐ Skirts
- ☐ Suits
- ☐ Sweaters
- ☐ Tuxedo

Footwear
- ☐ Athletic
- ☐ Leisure

- ☐ Dress
- ☐ Sandals/Flip flops
- ☐ Slippers

Outerwear
- ☐ Coats
- ☐ Jackets
- ☐ Gloves
- ☐ Hats
- ☐ Raincoat
- ☐ Scarves

Hygiene

Toiletries
- ☐ Bath gel
- ☐ Birth control
- ☐ Brush
- ☐ Comb
- ☐ Conditioner
- ☐ Contact Lenses & case
- ☐ Cotton balls
- ☐ Cotton swabs
- ☐ Curling Iron/Flat Iron

- ☐ Dental floss
- ☐ Deodorant
- ☐ Feminine Hygiene
- ☐ Hair dryer
- ☐ Insect repellent
- ☐ Lint roller
- ☐ Lip balm
- ☐ Medications
- ☐ Mirror
- ☐ Moisturizer
- ☐ Mouthwash

- ☐ Pain reliever
- ☐ Perfume
- ☐ Razor
- ☐ Saline solution
- ☐ Shampoo
- ☐ Sunscreen/block
- ☐ Tissue
- ☐ Toothbrush
- ☐ Toothpaste
- ☐ Tweezers
- ☐ Vitamins

Makeup
- ☐ Face cleanser
- ☐ Hand wipes
- ☐ Lip stick
- ☐ Makeup
- ☐ Nail clippers
- ☐ Nail file
- ☐ Nail polish
- ☐ Nail polish remover

Basic

Travel Aids
- ☐ Anxiety medication
- ☐ Bottled water
- ☐ Chewing gum
- ☐ Motion-sickness remedy
- ☐ Pleasure reading
- ☐ Sleeping mask
- ☐ Travel pillow
- ☐ Snacks

Other
- ☐ Directions
- ☐ First Aid Kit
- ☐ Journal
- ☐ Luggage tags
- ☐ Reservation info.
- ☐ Tickets
- ☐ Travel guides
- ☐ Travel locks
- ☐ Umbrella

Funds
- ☐ ATM card
- ☐ Cash
- ☐ Credit cards
- ☐ Money belt
- ☐ Plastic bags
- ☐ Travelers Checks
- ☐ Wallet

Around the World in Style ©Ariana Pierce

Packing List Continued

Tech Tools
- ☐ Batteries
- ☐ Battery/Juice Pack
- ☐ Car Charger
- ☐ Camera
- ☐ Camera Charger
- ☐ Cell phone
- ☐ Cell phone Charger
- ☐ Extension Cord
- ☐ Headphones
- ☐ Laptop
- ☐ Laptop Cord
- ☐ Nightlight
- ☐ Powerstrip
- ☐ Printer
- ☐ Tablet
- ☐ Tablet Cord
- ☐ Wall Jacks
- ☐ Voltage Adapters
- ☐ _____
- ☐ _____
- ☐ _____
- ☐ _____
- ☐ _____
- ☐ _____

Survival Kit
- ☐ Bobby Pins
- ☐ Business Cards
- ☐ Deodorant
- ☐ Eyelash Glue
- ☐ Flat shoes
- ☐ Magazine
- ☐ Note pad
- ☐ Pens
- ☐ Safety Pins
- ☐ Sewing Kit (small)
- ☐ Silk Hair Bonnet
- ☐ Silk Pillow Case (hair)
- ☐ Sticky Notes

Keep this kit packed and ready for travel at a moments notice.

Misc

Documents
- ☐ Copies of travel docs
- ☐ Copies of credit cards
- ☐ Copies of passport
- ☐ Drivers License
- ☐ Emergency contacts
- ☐ Medical cards
- ☐ Medical history
- ☐ List of Medications
- ☐ Passport & visas

Contacts
- ☐ Address book
- ☐ Business cards
- ☐ Calling cards
- ☐ Datebook

Laundry
- ☐ Laundry bag
- ☐ Laundry kit
- ☐ Sewing kit
- ☐ Stain remover
- ☐ Travel iron

Work
- ☐ Office Supplies
- ☐ Printer
- ☐ Work documents
- ☐ Work reading

Travel To-Do List

1.
2.
3.
4.
5.
6.
7.
8.
9.
10.
11.
12.
13.
14.
15.
16.

Notes & Ideas

Around the World in Style ©Ariana Pierce

How blessed all those in whom you live, whose lives become roads you travel. Psalm 84:5 Ksg

Around the World in Style ©Ariana Pierce

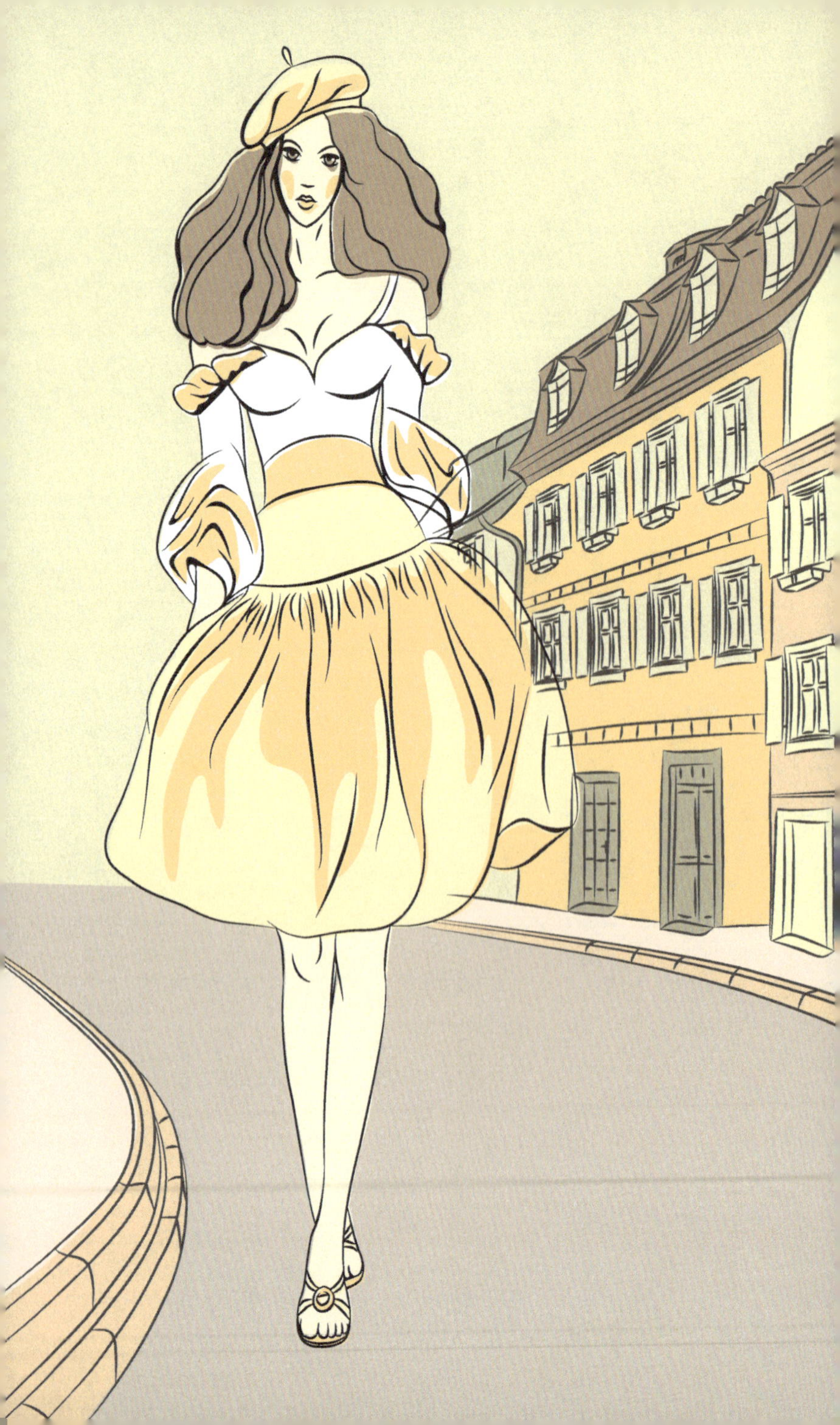

Around the World in Style ©Ariana Pierce

"I have wandered all my life, and I have also traveled; the difference between the two being this, that we wander for distraction, but we travel for fulfillment." - Hilaire Belloc

"Adventure is worthwhile." – Aristotle

Around the World in Style ©Ariana Pierce

# My Dream Trip Details

Use the space below to write the details about a trip you would like to take.

Destination: _____ **Travel Date:** _____

Itinerary

_____

Airline Used

_____

Hotel

_____

Restaurants

_____

Notes

Sites to See

Places to Go

Memorable
Moments

My Awesome
Adventures

Around the World in Style ©Ariana Pierce

My Dream Trip Vision Page

Use the space provided to paste pictures of your dream travel destination. Include places you'd like to visit, things you'd like to see and enjoy.

Destination:_____

Around the World in Style ©Ariana Pierce

Packing List

Destination:_____ Date: _____

Clothing

Accessories
- ☐ Belts
- ☐ Glasses & case
- ☐ Jewelry
- ☐ Sunglasses
- ☐ Ties
- ☐ Wristwatches

Basics
- ☐ Bras
- ☐ Pantyhose
- ☐ Robe

- ☐ Sleepwear
- ☐ Socks
- ☐ Tanks
- ☐ Undershirts
- ☐ Underwear

Casual
- ☐ Exercise wear
- ☐ Jeans
- ☐ Pants
- ☐ Shirts
- ☐ Shorts
- ☐ Swimsuits

- ☐ Tshirts

Dressy
- ☐ Dresses
- ☐ Dress shirts
- ☐ Skirts
- ☐ Suits
- ☐ Sweaters
- ☐ Tuxedo

Footwear
- ☐ Athletic
- ☐ Leisure

- ☐ Dress
- ☐ Sandals/Flip flops
- ☐ Slippers

Outerwear
- ☐ Coats
- ☐ Jackets
- ☐ Gloves
- ☐ Hats
- ☐ Raincoat
- ☐ Scarves

Hygiene

Toiletries
- ☐ Bath gel
- ☐ Birth control
- ☐ Brush
- ☐ Comb
- ☐ Conditioner
- ☐ Contact Lenses & case
- ☐ Cotton balls
- ☐ Cotton swabs
- ☐ Curling Iron/Flat Iron

- ☐ Dental floss
- ☐ Deodorant
- ☐ Feminine Hygiene
- ☐ Hair dryer
- ☐ Insect repellent
- ☐ Lint roller
- ☐ Lip balm
- ☐ Medications
- ☐ Mirror
- ☐ Moisturizer
- ☐ Mouthwash

- ☐ Pain reliever
- ☐ Perfume
- ☐ Razor
- ☐ Saline solution
- ☐ Shampoo
- ☐ Sunscreen/block
- ☐ Tissue
- ☐ Toothbrush
- ☐ Toothpaste
- ☐ Tweezers
- ☐ Vitamins

Makeup
- ☐ Face cleanser
- ☐ Hand wipes
- ☐ Lip stick
- ☐ Makeup
- ☐ Nail clippers
- ☐ Nail file
- ☐ Nail polish
- ☐ Nail polish remover

Basic

Travel Aids
- ☐ Anxiety medication
- ☐ Bottled water
- ☐ Chewing gum
- ☐ Motion-sickness remedy
- ☐ Pleasure reading
- ☐ Sleeping mask
- ☐ Travel pillow
- ☐ Snacks

Other
- ☐ Directions
- ☐ First Aid Kit
- ☐ Journal
- ☐ Luggage tags
- ☐ Reservation info.
- ☐ Tickets
- ☐ Travel guides
- ☐ Travel locks
- Umbrella

Funds
- ☐ ATM card
- ☐ Cash
- ☐ Credit cards
- ☐ Money belt
- ☐ Plastic bags
- ☐ Travelers Checks
- ☐ Wallet

Around the World in Style ©Ariana Pierce

Packing List Continued

Tech Tools
- ☐ Batteries
- ☐ Battery/Juice Pack
- ☐ Car Charger
- ☐ Camera
- ☐ Camera Charger
- ☐ Cell phone
- ☐ Cell phone Charger
- ☐ Extension Cord
- ☐ Headphones
- ☐ Laptop
- ☐ Laptop Cord
- ☐ Nightlight
- ☐ Powerstrip
- ☐ Printer
- ☐ Tablet
- ☐ Tablet Cord
- ☐ Wall Jacks
- ☐ Voltage Adapters
- ☐ _____
- ☐ _____
- ☐ _____
- ☐ _____
- ☐ _____

Survival Kit
- ☐ Bobby Pins
- ☐ Business Cards
- ☐ Deoderant
- ☐ Eyelash Glue
- ☐ Flat shoes
- ☐ Magazine
- ☐ Note pad
- ☐ Pens
- ☐ Safety Pins
- ☐ Sewing Kit (small)
- ☐ Silk Hair Bonnet
- ☐ Silk Pillow Case (hair)
- ☐ Sticky Notes

Keep this kit packed and ready for travel at a moments notice.

Misc

Documents
- ☐ Copies of travel docs
- ☐ Copies of credit cards
- ☐ Copies of passport
- ☐ Drivers License
- ☐ Emergency contacts
- ☐ Medical cards
- ☐ Medical history
- ☐ List of Medications
- ☐ Passport & visas

Contacts
- ☐ Address book
- ☐ Business cards
- ☐ Calling cards
- ☐ Datebook

Laundry
- ☐ Laundry bag
- ☐ Laundry kit
- ☐ Sewing kit
- ☐ Stain remover
- ☐ Travel iron

Work
- ☐ Office Supplies
- ☐ Printer
- ☐ Work documents
- ☐ Work reading

Travel To-Do List

1.
2.
3.
4.
5.
6.
7.
8.
9.
10.
11.
12.
13.
14.
15.
16.

Notes & Ideas

Around the World in Style ©Ariana Pierce

5 days
25 km
5×25=125 km

Ask where the good way is, and walk in it, and you will find rest for your souls. Jeremiah 6:16 NIV

Around the World in Style ©Ariana Pierce

Around the World in Style ©Ariana Pierce

The signposts of God are clear and point out the right road. The life-maps of God are right, showing the way to joy. Psalm 19:7-8 Msg

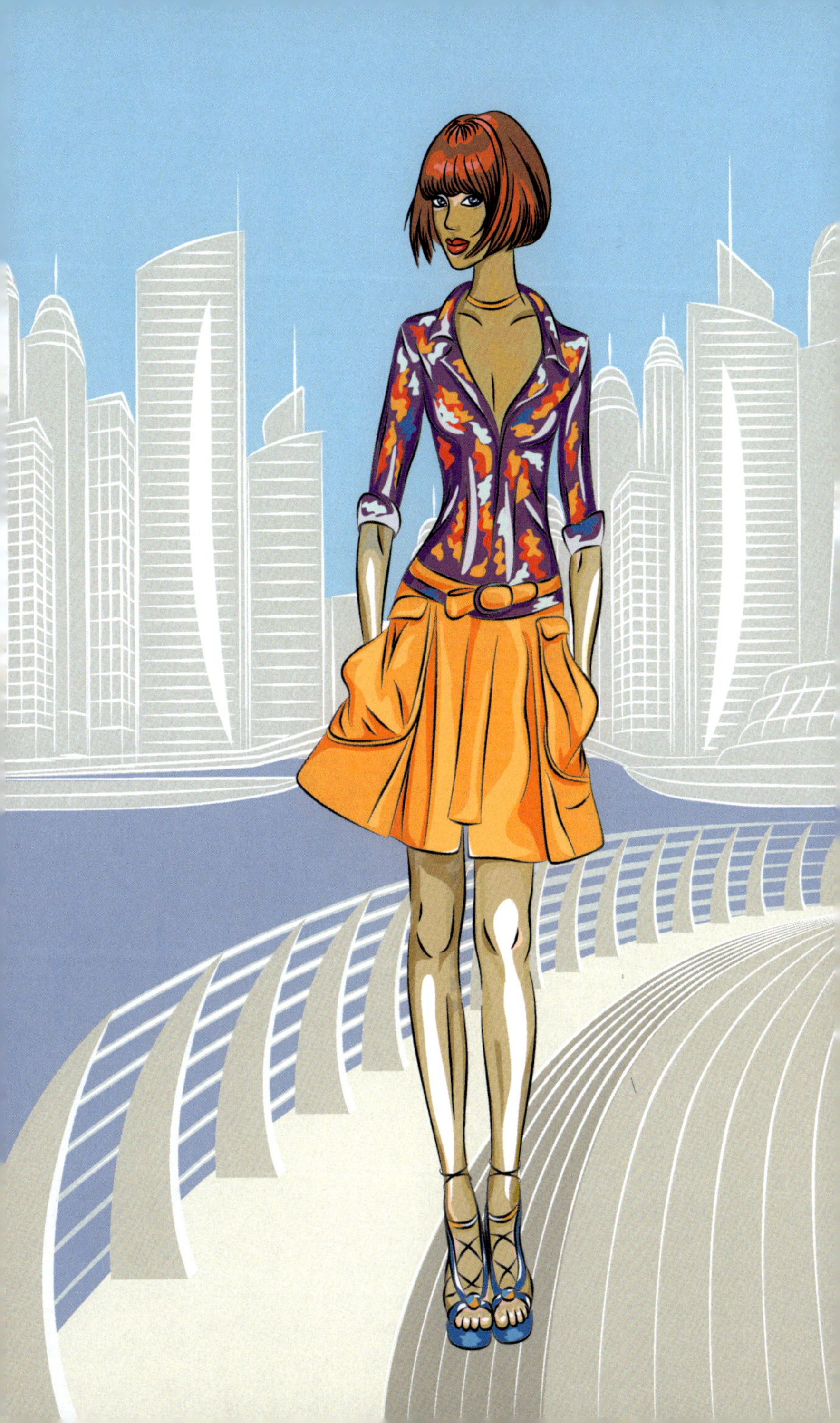

5 days
25 km
5×25=125 km

"I am a passionate traveler, and from the time I was a child, travel formed me as much as my formal education." - David Rockefeller

Around the World in Style ©Ariana Pierce

Around the World in Style ©Ariana Pierce

My Trip Details

Use the space below to write the details about a trip you've enjoyed.

Destination: _____ Travel Date: _____

Itinerary

Airline Used

Hotel

Restaurants

Notes

Sites I Saw

Places I Went

Memorable Moments

My Awesome Adventures

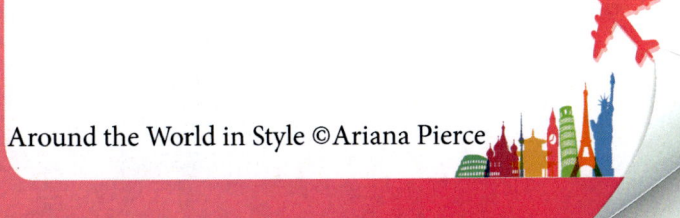

Around the World in Style ©Ariana Pierce

My Trip Scrapbook Page

Use the space provided to paste pictures and memorabilia of a travel destination you've visited.

Destination:

Around the World in Style ©Ariana Pierce

Packing List

Destination: _____ Date: _____

Clothing

Accessories
- ☐ Belts
- ☐ Glasses & case
- ☐ Jewelry
- ☐ Sunglasses
- ☐ Ties
- ☐ Wristwatches

Basics
- ☐ Bras
- ☐ Pantyhose
- ☐ Robe

- ☐ Sleepwear
- ☐ Socks
- ☐ Tanks
- ☐ Undershirts
- ☐ Underwear

Casual
- ☐ Exercise wear
- ☐ Jeans
- ☐ Pants
- ☐ Shirts
- ☐ Shorts
- ☐ Swimsuits

- ☐ Tshirts

Dressy
- ☐ Dresses
- ☐ Dress shirts
- ☐ Skirts
- ☐ Suits
- ☐ Sweaters
- ☐ Tuxedo

Footwear
- ☐ Athletic
- ☐ Leisure

- ☐ Dress
- ☐ Sandals/Flip flops
- ☐ Slippers

Outerwear
- ☐ Coats
- ☐ Jackets
- ☐ Gloves
- ☐ Hats
- ☐ Raincoat
- ☐ Scarves

Hygiene

Toiletries
- ☐ Bath gel
- ☐ Birth control
- ☐ Brush
- ☐ Comb
- ☐ Conditioner
- ☐ Contact Lenses & case
- ☐ Cotton balls
- ☐ Cotton swabs
- ☐ Curling Iron/Flat Iron

- ☐ Dental floss
- ☐ Deodorant
- ☐ Feminine Hygiene
- ☐ Hair dryer
- ☐ Insect repellent
- ☐ Lint roller
- ☐ Lip balm
- ☐ Medications
- ☐ Mirror
- ☐ Moisturizer
- ☐ Mouthwash

- ☐ Pain reliever
- ☐ Perfume
- ☐ Razor
- ☐ Saline solution
- ☐ Shampoo
- ☐ Sunscreen/block
- ☐ Tissue
- ☐ Toothbrush
- ☐ Toothpaste
- ☐ Tweezers
- ☐ Vitamins

Makeup
- ☐ Face cleanser
- ☐ Hand wipes
- ☐ Lip stick
- ☐ Makeup
- ☐ Nail clippers
- ☐ Nail file
- ☐ Nail polish
- ☐ Nail polish remover

Basic

Travel Aids
- ☐ Anxiety medication
- ☐ Bottled water
- ☐ Chewing gum
- ☐ Motion-sickness remedy
- ☐ Pleasure reading
- ☐ Sleeping mask
- ☐ Travel pillow
- ☐ Snacks

Other
- ☐ Directions
- ☐ First Aid Kit
- ☐ Journal
- ☐ Luggage tags
- ☐ Reservation info.
- ☐ Tickets
- ☐ Travel guides
- ☐ Travel locks
- Umbrella

Funds
- ☐ ATM card
- ☐ Cash
- ☐ Credit cards
- ☐ Money belt
- ☐ Plastic bags
- ☐ Travelers Checks
- ☐ Wallet

Around the World in Style ©Ariana Pierce

Packing List Continued

Tech Tools
- ☐ Batteries
- ☐ Battery/Juice Pack
- ☐ Car Charger
- ☐ Camera
- ☐ Camera Charger
- ☐ Cell phone
- ☐ Cell phone Charger
- ☐ Extension Cord
- ☐ Headphones
- ☐ Laptop
- ☐ Laptop Cord
- ☐ Nightlight
- ☐ Powerstrip
- ☐ Printer
- ☐ Tablet
- ☐ Tablet Cord
- ☐ Wall Jacks
- ☐ Voltage Adapters
- ☐ _____
- ☐ _____
- ☐ _____
- ☐ _____
- ☐ _____

Survival Kit
- ☐ Bobby Pins
- ☐ Business Cards
- ☐ Deoderant
- ☐ Eyelash Glue
- ☐ Flat shoes
- ☐ Magazine
- ☐ Note pad
- ☐ Pens
- ☐ Safety Pins
- ☐ Sewing Kit (small)
- ☐ Silk Hair Bonnet
- ☐ Silk Pillow Case (hair)
- ☐ Sticky Notes

Keep this kit packed and ready for travel at a moments notice.

Misc

Documents
- ☐ Copies of travel docs
- ☐ Copies of credit cards
- ☐ Copies of passport
- ☐ Drivers License
- ☐ Emergency contacts
- ☐ Medical cards
- ☐ Medical history
- ☐ List of Medications
- ☐ Passport & visas

Contacts
- ☐ Address book
- ☐ Business cards
- ☐ Calling cards
- ☐ Datebook

Laundry
- ☐ Laundry bag
- ☐ Laundry kit
- ☐ Sewing kit
- ☐ Stain remover
- ☐ Travel iron

Work
- ☐ Office Supplies
- ☐ Printer
- ☐ Work documents
- ☐ Work reading

Time Zones
Standard Time Zones of the World

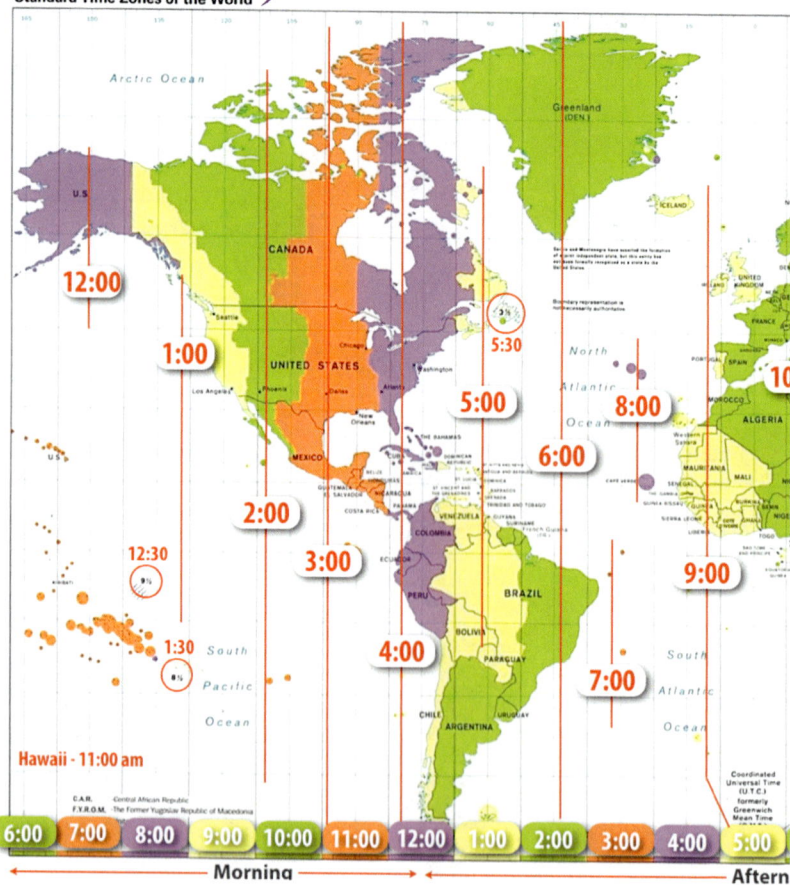

6:00	7:00	8:00	9:00	10:00	11:00	12:00	1:00	2:00	3:00	4:00	5:00

← Morning → ← Aftern

Hawaii - 11:00 am

C.A.R. Central African Republic
F.Y.R.O.M. The Former Yugoslav Republic of Macedonia

Coordinated Universal Time (U.T.C.) formerly Greenwich Mean Time

CALGARY — CANADA
NEW YORK — USA
LONDON — UNITED KINGDOM
BERLIN — GERMANY

MOSCOW
RUSSIA

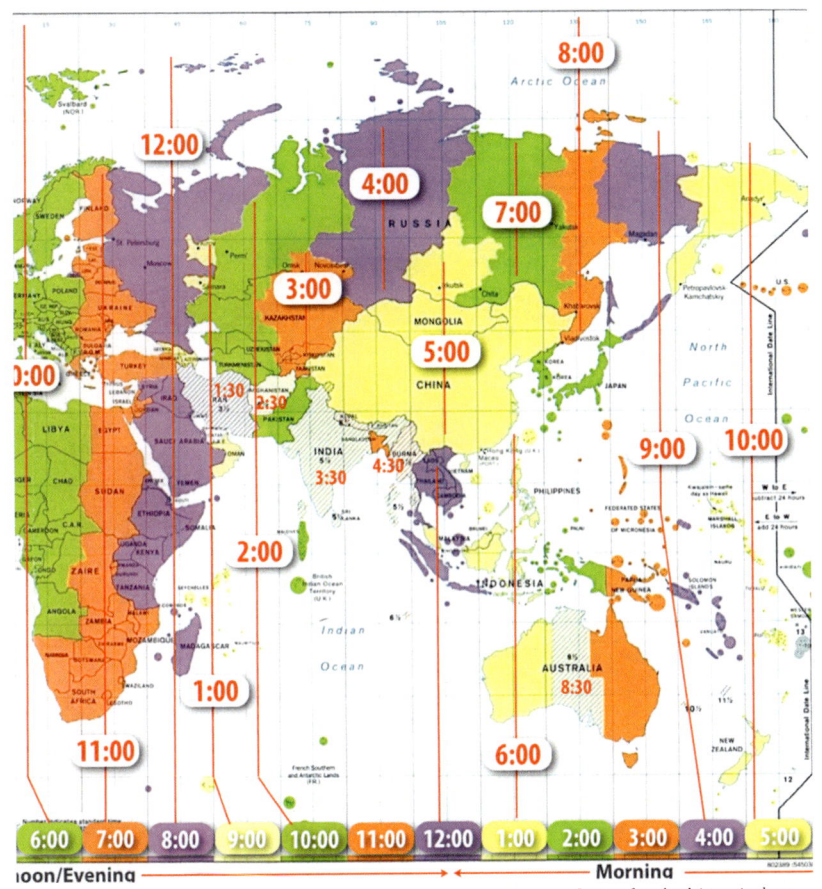

BEIJING
CHINA

TOKYO
JAPAN

I am with you and will keep you where ever you go.
Genesis 28:15

Around the World in Style ©Ariana Pierce

Around the World in Style ©Ariana Pierce

LONDON
NEW YORK
HONG KONG
LOS ANGELES
HONG KONG
VENICE
NEW YORK
MADRID
PARIS
PARIS
VENICE
DUBAI
LOS ANGELES
MIAMI
NEW YORK
MADRID
NICE
TOKYO
BUENOS AIRES
BUENOS AIRES
VENICE
SINGAPORE
TOKYO
MIAMI
NICE
NICE
VENICE
NICE
LOS ANGELES
LONDON
DUBAI
PARIS
HONG KONG
NICE
MADRID
NEW YORK
LONDON
NEW YORK
MIAMI
TOKYO
MADRID
TOKYO
ROME
SYDNEY
VENICE
SINGAPORE
MIAMI
HONG KONG
MADRID
SINGAPORE
MIAMI
DUBAI

Travel & Safety Tips

Reserve the Right: Reserve the right location. Double check the safety ratings in the area that you are making reservations in for lodging. Search travel websites such as TripAdvisor for reviews left by past guests.

Stash & Grab: Keep a stash of cash with you as well as some in a money pouch in the safe at your hotel. Store credit cards in a different location as well as a copy of your passport. On designated travel days, carry your passport in a separate location from your wallet or purse.

Stay Connected: Keep a charged cell phone with you at all times. Before leaving home, contact your service provider to determine if you have roaming capabilities or to set up an international data package. If the cost of the package outweighs your needs, just rent an inexpensive phone upon arrival. Other options include purchasing an international SIM card that can be used in unlocked GSM phones.

Alright Alone: When traveling alone, don't be afraid to venture out and explore the area. Stay alert, keep your common sense with you. Keep aware of your surroundings and the people that are in your immediate area. Don't get so focused on sight seeing that you miss what's going on around you.

Show & Tell: Make sure someone else always knows your schedule and detailed itinerary. Send destination and sight addresses and full details to more than one person. If you deviate, let your friends or family know. This way someone knows where you are and how you are getting there at all times.

Around the World in Style ©Ariana Pierce

Packing Hacks

Recycle:

Old sunglass cases can become cord storage.

Empty lip balm sticks can hide valuables such as cash or gem stones.

Square potholders are great for storing heated hair tools (flat iron etc.)

Binder clips can be used to wrap earbud cords and clip them to clothing.

Old shower caps work great to cover the soles of shoes (1 pair).

Use weekly pill cases to prevent thin jewelry from tangling.

Old contact lens cases are great for storing face cream or foundation.

Forgot your charger plug? The hotel room TV usually has a USB plug.

Keep it safe:

Cover eye shadow and other powdered cosmetics with a cotton pad.

Use plastic wrap between bottle tops for things like lotion or shampoo. Masking tape works well over the lid as well.

Roll clothes instead of folding for more space.

Around the World in Style ©Ariana Pierce

"The journey is the destination." - Dan Eldon

Made in the USA
San Bernardino, CA
23 February 2016